BETWEEN TWO SKIES

© Kay Cairns 2024

All rights reserved. Except for appropriate use in a book review, no part of this publication may be reproduced, stored in a retrieval system, or transmitted in any form or by any means, without the prior permission of the publisher, or in the case of photocopying or reprographic copying, a licence from the Copyright Agency of Australia.

BETWEEN TWO SKIES

ISBN 9780645797787

Walleah Press
South Launceston
Tasmania, Australia 7249

www.walleahpress.com.au
ralph.wessman@walleahpress.com.au

BETWEEN TWO SKIES

KAY CAIRNS

Contents

Discovering Australia   1
   Wacol Migrant Centre   3
   On Bidi Katitjiny Boardwalk   5
   Pinus Pinaster   6
   And yet there is beauty   7
   Vanishing Point   8
   By the Lake that Glistens   9
   On the Land of the Oor-dal-kalla People   10
   Through an Open Window   11
   On 'Big Water'   12
   The Space Below   13
   Night Sky   14
   Textures   15
   Morning   16
   Listening to Landscape   17
   Dalriada Dawn   18
   The Dry   19
   In the Wilderness   20
   Summer   21

Remembering Ireland   23
Summer Morning   25
Hinterland   26
In the Green Back Garden   27
Carrick Dhu   28
Torchie   29
Family Holiday   30
The Silken Wren   31
Night Watch   32
On Walking with my Brother   33
People Killed Each Other in the Place Where I was Born   34
Looking for the River   36
Return Flight   38
Mecca   40
Heart Beat   41
No Going Back   42
On a Country Lane   43
Back to the Garden   44
Bio   45
Acknowledgements   46

Discovering Australia

In the act of migration itself, imagination is infinite and the circumstances of the migratory move finite – creating a world of contradictions.
Irish President Michael D Higgins

Wacol Migrant Centre

Brisbane, Queensland 1983

From the wintered streets of Belfast
we land at a wooden stumpy
in the searing summer heat
of the outer city sticks.
Coats and boots dumped
in the first airport bin we find,
the air blowing through the taxi window like a hairdryer.
I wonder if it's safe to drink the water.

Vietnamese migrants flock round
to see my blonde daughter in her pram
and warn against the sun on her fair skin.
Days spent waiting, while the humidity
weighs on us, sticky as toffee,
and a possum in a tree frightens us
while walking in the cool of night.

At the hostel deli
we buy provisions and ice lollies
(icy poles they call them here),
a treat for the kids,
then feel the shame of allies
as the shopkeeper makes an Aboriginal boy wait
while he serves all the Whites.

But in this new country the sky is wide
with the fathomless infinity of space.
One evening we see a shooting star.

It is that we hold on to –
the conviction that under such a sky
change must come.

On Bidi Katitjiny Boardwalk

The light falls soft
between thin stalks
of ragged bodied barks.
Shadows slink
long and languid
across horizontal stripes
of warm wood decking.

On the air
wisps and whittles
float and fall,
as children's voices
descend in downward dreaming,
and disappear,
leaving only quiet birdsong
and a rush of wind.

Note: Bidi Katitjiny - Piney Lakes Wetlands, Perth, W.A. Before European settlement, a place where Noongar women held rituals and educated young children. Bidi - trail or pathway and Katitjiny - knowledge.

Pinus Pinaster

A woody aberration sits
grounded
on the flat unyielding plastic
of the table,
crusty bark petals
upturned, outpoured,
in blank defiance
of its alien context.

dnjong nih boordawan wangkinny

I inspect it
with all the blind insensitivity
of a visit to the zoo.

Note: Pinus Pinaster – *cluster pine;*
'*dnjong nih boordawan wangkinny*'
– *look, listen, talk later*

And yet there is beauty

in monochrome –
in the measured blur of light to dark
and black to grey,
a grey that has the reality and substance
that colour misses

and in the wind that breaks
the surface of the lake
into silver-splintered slivers,
ice-white reflections of an ash-bright sky

and in clouds,
not white, not black
but the artist's wash of somewhere in between,
all edges undefined
and smudging down
to sweep the wide, soft breast
of the earth.

Note: by Lake Joondalup, from 'Doondalup' – Noongar word meaning 'the lake that glistens', with reference to the dreamtime story of the Charnok woman.

Vanishing Point

Two white cockatoos
take off and fly beyond the trees
and I am reminded of my daughter
in her wedding white.

In the clear wash of morning,
the feather bodies sail,
seamless in a sweep and flow
of perfect diagonal tandem

and I am reminded
of her wedding dance
the sweep and sashay of her dress
in a perfect symmetry of steps.

The two birds fly, slim-lined
on the still swell of the air,
whiteness distilling
into a horizon
blue

By the Lake that Glistens

At the edge of the lake
the air reverberates with sound –
the muted fog-horn hoot, minor off-key plaintive
of a bird
calling its mate

and another –
the distant plink of piano notes
repeated
in a rhythm Arcadian
in its simplicity

yet it is quiet –
no Gershwin harmony of discordant metropolis,
here *just* harmony
minus the amphetamine rush
of onward onward onward

here still –
the low lake waters undulant on the breeze
and the growing green verdant
dotted and decked with slips and sips of colour,
sun-blaze orange, buttercup and Ophelia white
basking lovely
in a hush
of filtered light.

On the Land of the Oor-dal-kalla People

The path to the lake
is steep, pock-marked with ruts and rocks.
On either side, bush brims
with bird sounds
and the rustle of dried leaves
as lizards retreat.

Sometimes the wind sings in the trees
or kangaroos freeze
then spirit away.
One morning I found a copse of wildflowers,
butter-yellow and raspberry lolly-red.

They lit the earth for days.

Through an Open Window

a magpie wakes me
voice smooth-fluted
as cold water
falling
on rock.

I wait,
sound floating on air,
buoyant
as seawater.

Morning traffic passes
intermittent
and a dog barks, gruff,
across gardens.

In the gaps of silence
I wait,
hear only the unceasing ocean
of the city.

On 'Big Water'

I'm on the Ord again
and I am mesmerised
by breadth and depth
of sky and earth
where red strikes green,
strikes red,
then sifts again to blue.

Our boat cuts a slice
through the water
and I let myself be propelled
weightless
towards an ancient horizon.

*Note: 'big water' – indigenous name
for River Ord/Kununurra region*

The Space Below

Ningaloo Reef, Coral Bay, W.A.

In the opium prism of water
sight is amplified
and we drift
careless of sense and sound,
weightless.

Today a fluorescence of blue fish shines for us,
iridescent-electric in refracted light –
butterflies, flexing wings
in a euphoria of fluid space.

Night Sky

We stop on Gibb River Road
extinguish lights,
close quietly car doors.

Idle words
are silenced by the stillness,
thoughts melt into the night
as on this shallow disc of earth
the universe descends
to touch us.

Like anemones
we open outwards
to the stars.

Textures

South West, W.A.

Black stipple bark
burnt, stark,
amongst ochre-dyed, heat-dried leaves –
a million vermillion streaks
that scream
against the stretched blue brilliantine
of sky.

Morning

Soft light soaks
through horizontal lines
of blue white blinds.
Filtered haze of traffic
touches us only lightly
as we sleep.

Note: on the painting 'Snake Dreaming at Ngukalupalkarra 2002' – acrylic on linen by George Tjungurraeyi, Art Gallery WA

Listening To Landscape

Kelly's Knob, Kununurra, East Kimberley

It's our third year now,
third time we've made this journey.
I imagine myself still agile,
like a mountain goat, like her,
as I find flat red footholds in the rock,
ignore sharp grass spiking bare legs
and feet in thongs.

Clammy, like cellophane,
the night air wraps itself around us
while the sun in its descent
whispers a promise of relief.

The town below us stifles in the dying light,
sounds drift upwards, amplified by stillness.
From one house pumps Country and Western, then rap,
the same songs on repeat.
A woman's shrill profanity bites the air –
we watch a man stagger in the street.

On a blue-dusk horizon, ancient hills slumber,
breath rising quietly
as dreams ebb
away.

Dalriada Dawn

Neaves Road, Mariginiup, Perth, W.A.

I missed a picture-perfect moment the other day
in what's left of the forest.
The sun was rising at the time
and morning mist sat thick
as smoke off slack on a winter's fire,
so that all was caught and tangled-
became a faerie wood
where celestial light split thick wooded shafts
and was split and spilt itself
splintered, into myriad schisms of divinity.

And I wished I'd had a camera with me
to catch it, capture it, quarter and dice it,
to keep it fresh and bright
and as fundamental as it was.

The Dry

birds stifle
in the silence
of still trees
bark furls
leaves curl
dried husks slide,
skiffle and scuff
to crisp and crunch
underfoot,
or waft wafery away
on the bow wave
of the easterly.

In the Wilderness

*On visitors' responses to Boyd's 'Old Waterwheel',
Art Gallery of W.A.*

A sorry bunch -
each trying to outdo the other
with the 'right' interpretation
of the art.

Whites still reading white,
multiculturalists leaning left,
Boyd in the middle –
his message lost
on those who still see
only what they want to see.

Summer

It is hot again
and after gentle cooling
streets creak
in a white light intensity
that decimates urban murmurings
to make a desert sleep-scape
of the city.

Remembering Ireland

I suspected, however, that I wasn't homesick for anything I would find at home when I returned. The longing was for what I wouldn't find: the past and all the people and places there were lost to me.
Alice Steinbach

Summer Morning

South Sperrin, Dundonald, Belfast 1964

From deep child sleep
the unbroken drone of the lawnmower
wakes me
and cut grass coolness
seeps
through cotton curtains
of an open window.

Outside, the garden is wet with dew,
droplets wedged like liquid glass
in hearts of white carnations,
their ragged petals
stained
with ruby.

Hinterland

Strange dream I had
of wakening
to snow-bright light
of morning
I, a child again,
looking out
on the white-ice milk
of the garden.

Suburban infinite idyllic
where we children,
marauding Vikings,
bundled thick in woolen coats and scarves,
roamed the square

sliding
on black-white tyre-smooth snow

falling soft
in cotton kerbside drifts

playing till dark
in the nipping wet
of winter.

In the Green Back Garden

do you recall
the peg and bamboo high jump
where we scissor jumped
against the neighbourhood?

Young muscles launched us
and we sailed
slim limbed and weightless
into infinity.

Carrick Dhu

We fell asleep that night
lulled by the *tip* and *tap* of rain
on the caravan roof.

In the morning a hundred
holiday-makers, bright
in cotton tops and shorts,
stood in narrow doorways

faces upturned,
searching
for a gap in the grey.

*Note: Carrick Dhu caravan
park in Portrush, Antrim
Coast, N.I. circa 1965*

Torchy

For my mother

Milk bottles, sitting on the step.
Top inch of cream
beneath the silver cap.
You'd bring them in,
while we still slept,
on cold school mornings
in the dark,
or post-dawn days in summer
when the birds had been
and left their beak-prick punctures in the foil.

Now it's all plastic cartons
at the supermarket.
High this, low that,
extra calcium, no fat.
Where's Torchy now,
in his old Ford van,
milk bottles rattling in his big strong hands?
You drink your tea in a shrink-wrapped world,
us kids long gone…
with the cream.

Note: 'Torchy' a nickname my father gave the milkman, who delivered milk by torchlight on dark winter mornings. ('Torchy' – from the television jingle, 'Torchy the battery boy' circa 1959/60)

Family Holiday

weeks spent packing for the 'big safari', grand exodus to sun and sea in the overloaded Morris Minor, smell of melting tar, winding roads along a crumbling coastline, drinking fresh spring water that trickled down to the sea through pebbles white and smooth as birds' eggs, roast dinner on white linen tablecloths at Smith's dining hall in Larne, sandwiches and flasks of tea, icy swims, sheltering on the Miami blanket behind a rainbow coloured windbreaker, feet in warm rock pools, sleeping in the caravan at night, sand still between our toes, the deep roll of the ocean in our ears.

The Silken Wren

I used to watch my father
at our dining table, working on designs
for tablecloths and tea-towels
made by the textile company where he worked.

With a fine brush, dipped in matt brown paint
that smelt of linseed, his hand moved skilfully,
filling the space between the lines
on translucent sheets of tracing paper.

Sometimes the images were of flowers,
sometimes cottages, kittens, puppies with large eyes –
always inoffensive subjects we'd now regard as kitsch.
But at the time I saw him as an artist.

I'd heard my mother call his firm the *Silken Wren*
and I imagined small birds,
worked in layers of silk resplendence,
with all the phantasmagorical, allegorical colours of the East,
exotic and poetic as Khayyam's verses,
my father the grand vizier, his talents sought
both far and wide.

It was only later, when he died
that I discovered the name was not the *Silken Wren*,
but the sadly more prosaic *Silk and Rayon*.
The loss to me was so much more than mispronunciation.

Night Watch

Like crystal lace
frozen patterns grow
on black-night glass.
From the North
wind blows bitter.

I light the lamp
push out chill with amber,
watch my child sleep.

On Walking with my Brother

Belfast Hills, 2018

The weather turned, that day we went up Cave Hill.
The blue-ice glitter of an Irish sun disintegrated
as upland heaths and grasslands were submerged
in a sodden clothesline of an afternoon.

The front set in as we climbed,
a blanket of damp closing out the view
but in your world of childhood past
you had forgotten geography and meteorology.

We carried on, you talking fast,
the years of absence creating a frantic sled ride
of memories now released,
for perhaps the thickening mist and misle lent themselves
to that fond *recherche* of *temps perdu*.

But it was on that day,
in the ancient landscape of the chieftains,
that I knew you were no longer the leader
but the lost.

People Killed Each Other in the Place Where I was Born

After witnessing the Orange Order centennial march in Belfast, May 2022

It was 1969
when the army moved in.
Leaning on the back of the settee
in the window of the good front room,
we watched the troop carriers and armoured cars
roll up the hill from Belfast.

It didn't seem that long ago
since we'd roamed the hayfields of the green belt,
watched combine harvesters slice yellow stalks to stubble,
picked wads of soft grey putty
from the window frames of new-built homes.

But when 'the strike' came
my mother said it probably wasn't safe
for my Catholic friend to visit us again.

They say that things are better now
yet if I go out in my pink *Celtic* cap
my brother tells me I'll 'get killed'
and when the bands march in July
my friend stays indoors
while her husband threatens to tear down the orange flag
that's been hoisted on a pole outside their house.

It's still there, all these months later,
tattered by the autumn winds and rain,
and I wonder if I'll ever visit home again.

Note: 1969 – the year the British army moved into Northern Ireland at the beginning of 'the troubles'; 'strike' – the UWC (Ulster Workers' Council) strike of 1974, responsible for bringing down the power-sharing Northern Ireland Assembly and Executive and a return to Direct Rule from Westminster.

Looking for the River

For my brother

We're in the street,
where the old Astoria once stood,
and it's late afternoon and nearly dark
when he tells me he went looking for the river
where we caught fish and frogspawn –
taking them home in buckets,
forgetting them when they died.

And although the place is different now
(for nothing stays the same...or only in our minds)
he'd found a way in, through the dog rose, thorns and nettles,
the burdening, brambling overgrowth of the years.
And there's an excitement in his voice –
like a boy on the brink of a great adventure,
that *Boys' Own* journey to the source of all secrets, all life.

We talk of his writing,
the plan to write the novel, condensed now
to the more urgent target of one hundred pages,
each page to be imbued with sun and snow, fields and football,
all the icons of the past, mythologised
into a narrative both lyrical and pastoral, epic and mystic,
in the grand and tragical sweep of its conception.

Streetlights blink on,
push back against the growing blackness,
and the air contracts around us
with the bone-deep cold of winter.
When we hug, I feel the thinness of his arms.
It's a long hug,
the kind that lets you know it's probably our last.

Return Flight

I fly over the house just after take-off,
headphones filtering classical,
like Mum on the piano.

I imagine Dad there,
see his face,
younger than before he died
but older than his black-haired prime
when he was the swimmer.

His culture lies around him –
not the art he dabbled in,
before painting the backyard orange
like the sun,
but in the hard cash of engine parts
and old cars bought cheap,
fixed up to sell in the paper o.n.o.

Years he spent, laid out
in the concrete alleyway,
fingers and hands ingrained with oil and grease,
cold as the war that dumped him,
damaged, back at home;
cold, and wet,
and a wind whistling always
through the ragged woollen jumper that he wore.

That's where I leave them –
Mum, clean and classical,
Dad, fingers in the muck,
still trying to find a way out of the trenches.

Mecca

This is the first time I have made
the pilgrimage to the house where I was born
without my brother.
Each year, on my return,
we'd, take the walk along the brambled track
(*the railer* as we called it)
and up the muddy lane.

The roses and carnations
planted by my father
have long since died away,
but still I see myself a child,
looking out on the street,
and I remember each December
when our tree stood in that front room,
its lights diffused nebulae
seeping colour
through black-wet window glass.

Heart Beat

I am bound in dark deep,
buried
by choke of bog –
reverberation of air and light
dulled
by eons of aged matter
not yet brittled.

Here peat, still pliant, cradles flesh
that waits
for the high-hawk cry of the uilleann pipe,
when earth will open
and blackened feet will dance
to the low-tone timbre and heart-deep beat
of the bodhrán.

No Going Back

I've been back a week now
and I keep thinking
about how my brother and I
argued, gently,
about what we were.

He staunchly clinging
to the identity of the 'Ulster Scot',
I, exile and turncoat,
harking back to an Ireland
I never really knew.

I read Glenn Patterson's *'Lapsed Protestant'*
and the Odyssey, big Samson and Goliath,
rise up from crude Neanderthal drawings
of King Billy and the balaclava'd man.

But Patterson's love of Belfast
is matched only by my brother's.
Give me Dublin any day,
even if it isn't mine,
for I can't for the life of me
love Belfast.

Note: '*Lapsed Protestant*' – *book by Glenn Patterson, Northern Ireland 2006; Samson and Goliath – twin shipbuilding gantry cranes; Odyssey – sports and entertainment complex located in the Titanic Quarter.*

On a Country Lane

Strangford Lough, Ards Peninsula

Winter light trickles
across the lough
as afternoon sun melts
into the lip of the Earth.

Hedgerow thickets are lush
with red haws of hawthorn
and the season's last blackberries.

A bower of wildness cloaks my way;
gives the yellow-beaked blackbird dark refuge
as it darts amongst foliage
in smouldering light.

Back to the garden

A memory of home

A squat black bumble bee burrows
into a dense head of butter-lustre petals,
and it is the fecundity of Ireland
in the depth of coat, like fur, suckling
a bursting girth of yellow.

And although there was always the grey,
I remember only this burgeoning brim of colour –
thick carmine cloth of tulip,
pink-clustered crush of rose,
and rippled clot of cream carnation,
as flowers loll, lazy indolent,
over garden walls.

Kay Cairns | Bio

Now living in Perth WA, Kay Cairns is an Irish born poet who grew up in 1970s Belfast during 'the Troubles'. During that time she studied English, French and Russian literature at Queen's University of Belfast, where she was fortunate to have had the opportunity to attend readings by poets Seamus Heaney and Yevgeny Yevtushenko.

Kay emigrated to Australia in 1983 and began writing 'for real' during her long service leave from teaching in 2001. She began by writing fiction, but in 2003 began to write poetry. Her first poem, *Exit Wounds*, written after attending a Juice writing retreat workshop run by the late Andrew Burke, went on to win the Tom Collins Poetry Prize in 2004. In 2023 Kay received a commendation in the same competition with her poem *Looking for the River*, and her poem *Wacol Migrant Centre* was highly commended in the Spilt Ink Poetry competition 2018.

Kay's poetry has been published in *Quadrant* and in Australian poetry anthologies such as *Famous Reporter, Poetica Christi, Indigo, The Weighing of the Heart, Poetry D'Amour, Tempus, Locus, Cuttlefish* and most recently *Brushstrokes* and the *Liquid Amber Poetry of Home* anthology. She also presents creative writing and poetry workshops at Peter Cowan Writing Centre and has been guest poet and regular open mic reader at WOW (Walking on Water, 2005), Supper Club and Voicebox.

In her poetry Kay draws on strong emotional relationships with people and places, aspects of the natural world often triggering connections with life experiences. Her poems also explore political or cultural themes and her relationship with Australia and with her country of birth.

Acknowledgements

'Wacol Migrant Centre' and 'Night Sky' were previously published in Locus – OOTA Anthology 2019

'Wacol Migrant Centre' was also previously published in Brushstrokes IV – W.A. Poets Publishing 2023

'Hinterland' was previously published in Inner Child – Poetica Christi Press 2015

'Return Flight' was previously published in Poetry of Home, Liquid Amber Prize Anthology, 2023

'Vanishing Point' was previously published in Indigo Issue 1, Out of the Asylum journal 2007

www.ingramcontent.com/pod-product-compliance
Lightning Source LLC
Chambersburg PA
CBHW032018290426
44109CB00013B/706

*9 7 8 0 6 4 5 7 9 7 7 8 7 *